Up in Smoke

A Guide to Cigar Basics

★ **POWERLINE PUBLISHING CO.** ★

Special Thanks to
Rob Chirico
for his research
and skillful writing.
Cheers, Rob!

Acknowledgments
—Cover Design and Layout by Pearl & Associates, Inc.

Copyright © 1998 Powerline Publishing Co.
All rights reserved.
Printed in U.S.A.
ISBN 0-942320-61-1

Powerline Publishing Co.
3600-K South Congress Avenue
Boynton Beach, FL 33426
800-367-9388

TABLE OF CONTENTS

Introduction 5
The Cigar in History 6
Cigar Tobaccos From Around The World 7
Growing Tobacco 10
The Perfect Blend 11
Aging the Cigar 12
Well-Known Brands of Cigars 13
Picking The Perfect Cigar 15
Understanding Cigar Parts 16
Spanish 101 17
Size Doesn't Matter 18
The Band! 19
Choose Your Weapon 20
Off With Its Head 21
Lighting A Cigar! 22
Holding Your Cigar Like A Pro! 23
Character Traits 24
Saying The Right Thing 25
Cigar Storage 26
Glossary of Cigar Terms 27

> "*I have made it a rule never to smoke more than one cigar at a time.*"
>
> —Mark Twain

INTRODUCTION

"*If I cannot smoke in heaven, I shall not go.*"

Mark Twain admitted to buying only the cheapest cigars, but his quips about smoking are priceless. As adamant as Twain could be about cigar smoking, he is in good company. When we conjure up images of Sigmund Freud, Winston Churchill, Groucho Marx, Orson Welles, or even Roger Rabbit's feisty little friend, Baby Henry, their portraits would be incomplete without a prominent cigar. Like the people who brandished them, cigars have been cherished and damned. There is nothing neutral about a good cigar.

The U.S. trade embargo with Cuba, coupled with negative statistics about cigarettes, reduced cigar smoking to a smoldering ember over the next two decades. But — along with its sophisticated cousin, the Martini — the mystique, allure and inestimable pleasure derived from the stately stogie is enjoying a fiery comeback. Our hope is that this volume will help inspire the new generation of men and women to celebrate the magical indulgence of the "ritual of lighting up."

THE CIGAR IN HISTORY

By the turn of the century, cigar production and sales in the U.S. were at a level that has never been surpassed. Cigars made entirely from Cuban tobacco were called "clears." Their outrageous price of nearly 20 cents a piece in 1919 prompted Vice President Thomas Marshall to exclaim the often repeated words, "What this country needs is a good-five cent cigar." Whereas machine rollers eventually did make cheaper cigars readily available, they never challenged the quality of hand-rolled cigars.

Americans smoked 3.5 billion cigars last year, more than any other nationality except the Chinese.

CIGAR TOBACCOS FROM AROUND THE WORLD

Cuba

Because of its ideal climate and superlative soil, Cuba produces what is regarded as the finest filler tobacco in the world. Cuba's best tobacco-growing area is on the west side of the island, in Pinar del Río. Typically, Cuban tobacco is strong and full-bodied, with a rich aroma. Most factories of premium hand-rolled cigars are located in or around Havana.

The Dominican Republic

Although Cuba has suffered under the U.S. trade embargo, its neighbor to the east, the Dominican Republic, has flourished. It produces a great variety of quality cigar tobaccos, used mostly for filler and binder. The primary growing region is near the northern city of Santiago. Most of the Dominican Republic's tobacco is derived from Cuban-seed varieties. While not as strong as its Cuban ancestor, it is quite full-flavored and lends itself to the creation of unusually complex blends.

Honduras/Nicaragua

Honduras and Nicaragua grow high-quality Cuban-seed filler and Connecticut-seed wrapper tobaccos. But both countries have had setbacks. Honduras has suffered from periodic tobacco mold infestations, and Nicaragua's tobacco regions have yet to recover from a 10-year civil war. Both countries produce a robust tobacco with rich and aromatic flavors.

Mexico

Unlike other countries that may rely upon wrapper or filler imports, most cigars produced in Mexico are made entirely with native tobacco. Mexican tobacco is generally used as filler and binder for cigars, and the Sumatra seed cultivated in the San Andres Valley provides a formidable nut-brown maduro wrapper.

United States

The sandy soil found in the Connecticut River Valley, just north of Hartford, is responsible for some of the finest, and most expensive, wrapper leaf tobacco in the world. Connecticut Shade is the fine brown to brownish-yellow leaf whose elasticity and superior burning quality have made it a source of premium wrapper leaves. Another leaf, Connecticut Broadleaf, is a much darker and more heavily veined leaf. It is used primarily on maduro-style cigars.

Africa

Cameroon, in West Africa, manufactures high-quality wrapper leaf. Cameroon's tobacco is derived from Sumatra seed. The leaf produces a medium-body smoke, which complements full-flavored filler tobaccos. Cameroon wrappers are greenish-brown to dark brown. The distinct grain of this wrapper is referred to as its "tooth."

Indonesia

Sumatra-variety tobacco comes from the various islands making up Indonesia. Sumatra wrapper leaves are usually dark brown, but not overly assertive. Most of the wrapper leaf grown there is used in the making of small cigars. Brazil is a major importer of Sumatra leaf.

Philippines

In an attempt to rival Cuban cigars, La Flor, the biggest cigar company in the Philippines, hired cigar master Alfredo Salinas to train its rollers classic Cuban methods. The tobacco is generally mild and aromatic, and the Philippines hope to capture a world market through their refined techniques.

"...I promised myself that if ever I had some money that I would savor a cigar each day after lunch and dinner. This is the only resolution of my youth that I have kept, and the only realized ambition which has not brought dissillusion."
-Somerset Maugham

GROWING TOBACCO

The growing of tobacco and the subsequent making of cigars is a lengthy and laborious process. Good tobacco needs very loose soil, and fields are plowed numerous times to this end. Seeds are small - one teaspoon can provide six acres - so they must be started in carefully tended flat ground. After about six weeks of germination, the seedlings reach roughly eight inches and are ready for transplanting to the field. During the next six weeks, the plants are visited hundreds of times to watch for disease and to trim buds and shoots - or "suckers." Corojo plants, grown under muslin cheesecloth called a tapado, are protected from the sun's rays. This delicate tobacco leaf is used for the cigar's wrapper. Unlike the corjo, the criollo plant thrives under full sunlight, producing several varieties of leaf that are blended for the filler as well as for the inner binder, which keeps the filler intact.

It takes another six weeks before cigar tobacco is harvested and reaches the curing barns, or casas del tabaco. Here the tobacco is raised on poles for drying, also known as air curing. The first fermentation stage then begins as workers pile slightly moistened tobacco in huge bales or stacks. Temperatures inside the bales reach as high as $140°$ as the cigar "sweats" during the early stages of fermentation. Some tobacco may be "turned" and restacked up to three or four times. There is an intermediary moistening - moja - before the final fermentation. This process releases ammonia, lowers nicotine and generally mellows the tobacco. Leaves are air-dried on racks and packed in burlap bales called tercisos. After aging from 18 months to two years - and in some cases as long as 10 years - the tobacco is ready for blending.

THE PERFECT BLEND

Tobacco Blending

A cigar blend is created by a master blender. An alchemist of sorts, he combines tobaccos of varying tastes and strengths to create a unique balance for an exceptional smoke. Depending on size, or ring gauge, a cigar may contain from two to four different tobaccos. The specific blend of tobacco leaf is brought to the galeria of the factory. The blender places his special formula in different boxes at the roller's desk, and the magical process continues.

Rolling

The roller, or torcedore, takes whole leaves for the filler and gathers them on a binder, a flat, elastic leaf of tobacco. Any torn leaves or shreds are used for cigarettes. He rolls them all together into a "bunch," and then places them in the bottom half of a wooden mold. The sizes of molds are determined by the type of cigar being made. Once the worker has used a screw press to compact the cigar, he returns the wooden molds to the rolling tables. The roller removes the bunch from the mold and wraps it with a scrupulously chosen wrapper leaf that has been handcut to the appropriate size. Keeping the right pressure on the leaves, the roller stretches the wrapper around them. Using a flavor-enhanced vegetable paste, the wrapper is fastened. An experienced roller may produce more than 100 cigars a day. Allowed to smoke while he or she performs the slow and exacting task, the meticulous torcedores listen to a reader who recites the latest news, sports or maybe even a juicy novel.

Presently, there are six million cigar smokers in the U.S., of which approximately one million are premium cigar smokers.

AGING THE CIGAR

Once the cigar has been carefully inspected, it enters the aging room. A cigar is aged for at least three weeks, but some makers will age their brands for as much as 180 days. This allows the different cigar tobaccos to develop the marvelous blend that will afford a completely balanced smoking experience. A fine cigar may also inspire a glorious transcendent moment. As George Sand aptly put it, "The cigar numbs sorrow and fills the solitary hours with a million gracious images."

"I drink a good deal, sleep little, and smoke cigar after cigar. That is why I am in 200 percent shape."
-Winston Churchill

WELL-KNOWN BRANDS OF CIGARS

Any brand of cigar may have numerous types of cigars produced under its label. Cohiba produce Coronas Especial, Espledido, Exquisito, Panatela and so forth. To complicate matters, after the institution of the Cuban embargo, families left Cuba and established firms in other countries. You may find a Cohiba Robusto from Cuba as well as from the Dominican Republic. The following is a list of popular brands, accompanied by their place of origin.

Arturo Fuente — Dominican Republic
Ashton — Dominican Republic
Avo Uvezian — Dominican Republic
Bauzà — Dominican Republic
Bering — Honduras
Bolívar — Dominican Republic

Cohiba — Cuba and Dominican Republic
Davidoff — Dominican Republic
Don Diego — Dominican Republic
Don Juan — Nicaragua
Don Lino — Honduras
Don Tomàs — Honduras

Don Urquijo — Philippines
Dunhill — Dominican Republic
Fonseca — Cuba and Dominican Republic
Griffen's — Dominican Republic

WELL-KNOWN BRANDS OF CIGARS
CONTINUED

H. Upmann — Cuba and Dominican Republic
Henry Clay — Dominican Republic
Hoyo de Monterrey — Cuba and Honduras
Joya de Nicaragua — Nicaragua
Juan Clemente — Dominican Republic
La Gloria Cubana — Cuba and United States
La Flor — Philippines
La Plata — Honduras
Macanudo — Dominican Republic and Jamaica
Montecristo — Cuba
Montecruz — Dominican Republic
Nat Sherman — Dominican Republic
Partagas — Cuba and Dominican Republic
Paul Garmirian — Dominican Republic
Pleiades — Dominican Republic
Punch — Cuba and Dominican Republic
Romeo y Julieta — Cuba and Dominican Republic
Savinelli — Dominican Republic
Temple Hall — Jamaica
Troya — Dominican Republic
Zino — Honduras

PICKING THE PERFECT CIGAR

A few general rules of thumb that you should know before you open the humidor's door for the first time...

1) A cigar needs to be stabilized in a humidor after shipment. Look for the open boxes that have been there for awhile. If you're not sure put your choice in your humidor at home for a week or so to stabilize it properly.

2) A good cigar should be even and smooth and should "give" but not be too soft. Look for lumps or soft spots by squeezing gently up and down the body. Be careful, even if that cigar doesn't feel right to you somebody else might buy it – so don't damage it!

3) Look closely for any discoloration, cracks or looseness in the wrapper.
A good wrapper should be tight and smooth and consistent in color.

"The best cigar in the world is the one you prefer to smoke on special occasions, enabling you to relax and enjoy that which gives you maximum pleasure." -Zino Davidoff

UNDERSTANDING CIGAR PARTS

Wrappers

A cigar's wrapper is the outside layer of tobacco that holds the cigar together. It is also the primary source of a cigar's flavor. The wrapper is usually the highest quality leaves, and is available in a variety of colors from lightest, Double Claro to the very dark, Oscuro.

Filler

Filler tobacco makes up the inner body of a cigar. The filler leaves determine the strength of a cigar. There are two types of filler; short filler, remnants and small pieces of tobacco, and long filler, which is made of single leaves bunched together.

Binders

Binder leaves are the leaves that are used to bind the bunch of filler tobacco together. Binders can be made of single whole leaves or tobacco remnants held together with glue or other substances.

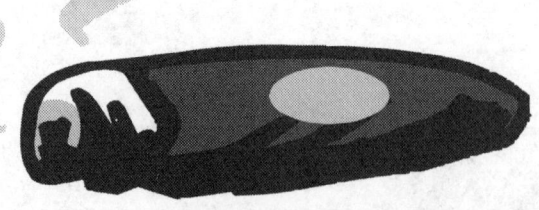

SPANISH 101...
UNDERSTANDING CIGAR STYLES

There are two basic broad shape categories
that fit all cigars:
Parejos, any cigar with straight sides
Figurados, all "irregular" shaped cigars.

Parejos can be divided into three basic subcategories based on the relative proportion of their dimensions.

1) Coronas (including Coronas, Double Coronas, Presidentes, Robustos, and Churchills). Their open "foot" and a rounded "head" characterize all Coronas.
2) Panatelas are longer than Coronas and are generally much thinner.
3) Lonsdales and thicker than Panatelas and longer than Coronas.

Figurados are a little easier to define. There are generally four subcategories of Figurados.

1) Belicoso is the smallest. These small tapered cigars have a rounded head and a larger foot.
2) Pyramids are next, tapering from a large foot to a small head. A true Pyramid has a pointed, not a round, head. Many smokers call a large Pyramid a Torpedo, yet a true Torpedo has a large foot, smaller, pointed head and slight bulge in the middle.
3) Perfectos are tapered on both ends to be smaller on the ends than the wider middle section – the classic "cigar shape".
4) Diademas is the giant of the cigar world. These cigars are 8 inches or longer.

SIZE DOESN'T MATTER...

UNDERSTANDING CIGAR SIZES

Here is a list of standard sizes. The first dimension is the length of the cigar in inches. The second is the ring gauge of the cigar.

- BELICOSO ....6.5" x 52
- CHURCHILL ....7" x 47
- CORONA...5.5" x 42
- CORONA GORDA ....6-6.5" x 52
- CORONA GRANDE ....6-6.5" x 46-50
- CORONA LARGA ....6.5" x 46-50
- CORONA MAJOR ....6" x 44-46
- DEMITASSE ....3.5" – 5.25" x 26-50
- DOUBLE CORONA ....7.5"-8.5" x 49-52
- GIGANTE ....7-7.5" x 54-60
- LONG PANATELA ....6.75"-7.75" x 30-38
- LONSDALE ....6.5" x 42
- LONSDALE GRANDE ....6.5"-7" x 44
- PANATELA ....5"-6.5" x 28-38
- PARODI ....3.5" x 36
- PERFECTO ....tapered head and foot
- PETIT CORONA ....5" x 40-42
- PRESIDENTE ....7.5"-8" x 52
- PYRAMID ....6" tapered head to oversized foot
- ROBUSTO ....6" x 45-50
- ROBUSTO GRANDE ....6.5" x 48-50
- ROTHSCHILD ....4.5"-5.5" x 48-50
- THIN PANATELA ....5"-6.5" x 24-26
- TOSCANI ....7" x 36

THE BAND!

To remove or not remove a cigar's band... that is the question.

This silly yet major decision is yours and yours alone, and is solely a matter of personal choice, unless you are in Britain, where it is a must to remove a cigar's band.

If you're removing the band, wait until after you have lit the cigar, allowing the warmth to soften things up, making removal less likely to damage the wrapper.

If you want to smoke your cigar with the band on, remember that if you smoke down far enough you'll be forced to either remove it or smoke the band too!

A note of etiquette...

Socially speaking, those who keep the band on while they smoke are perceived to be showing off.

"Sometimes a cigar is just a cigar."
-Sigmund Freud

CHOOSE YOUR WEAPON...

THE CUTTER

Nature's Own Cutters... Your Teeth

Use this ancient method if you don't have any other cutting device and you're not out to impress. Bite firmly on both sides of the head of your cigar – then find a private place to spit out the cap.

Guillotine Cutters

Most single-blade cutters of this variety will do a very poor job of cutting your cigar, resulting in split, smashed or tattered cuts. Cut quickly and decisively.

Punch Cutters

.44 Magnums are very easy to use, making a perfect round opening in a cigar's cap. Some will actually remove the cut piece of cap. Punch style cutters are a good choice to take the fear out of cutting.

V-Cut Clippers

This style is also easy to use as it automatically determines the length and position of the cut. Depending on the size of the "v", this style is not very adaptable, however, to varying sizes and styles of cigars.

OFF WITH ITS HEAD...

CUTTING YOUR CIGAR

Cutting a cigar is intimidating at first... where to cut? Which cutter is best? Will I unravel the wrapper and end up with a mouth full of tobacco?

Here is a foolproof method...

First, examine your cigar. Almost all cigars have a "cap" on the closed end or "head". The cap is a bit of tobacco used to close off the head – you will be able to see how far down the length of the cigar the cap goes.

Wherever the cap stops is your cutting limit! Cut beneath the cap's line and your cigar will start to unravel. Trying to smoke an unraveling cigar is not a pleasant experience!

"Any cigar smoker is a friend because I know what he feels."

-Alfred de Musset

LIGHTING A CIGAR!

Step #1: "Toasting the Foot"

Hold the flame to the outside edge of the foot (end) and rotate the cigar to evenly toast the edge. This method will allow the sulfur created from the burn to wear off into the air instead of in your mouth.

Step #2: "Draw Partner"

Hold a large flame about a half-inch from the cigar and rotate the cigar as you draw in air. Your draw will pull the flame in toward the cigar. The turning will allow for an even burn.

Step #3: "Puff"

Slowly rotate and puff your cigar naturally. Don't inhale! Draw smoke into your mouth smoothly and release the smoke slowly and steadily. Relax and enjoy!. A puff or two a minute is all it takes to keep your cigar lit.

Step #4: "Flicking Your Ash"

Allow a cigar's ashes to get approximately 1 inch long before you flick it. A longer ash helps to keep cool the smoke you inhale. The longer, cooler ash will also improve the taste of your cigar.

HOLDING YOUR CIGAR LIKE A PRO!

Unless you're European, don't hold your cigar like a cigarette. The proper way to hold a cigar is between your second and third fingers.

NOW...
IT'S TIME FOR A DRINK

The best time to enjoy a premium cigar is after a good, but not too filling, meal. Smoking a cigar on an empty stomach will allow the bad effects of nicotine to make it into you system, creating nausea and making an enjoyable time into a bad experience.

Enhancing your cigar experience with a beverage can be an added delight. Beer, bourbon, brandy, cognac, espresso, port, scotch and wine are all prime choices, depending on your mood and personal preferences of course.

CHARACTER TRAITS

A premium cigar that is rolled well and packed nicely will burn slowly and evenly. The ash can grow, without flicking of course, to two or even three inches in length without bending or breaking.

A really fine quality cigar can usually be smoked down to the nub without becoming bitter in flavor. If you notice a change in taste, give your cigar a rest in its ashtray. Your cigar may have encountered a spot of tar that needs to burn off and may return to its smooth flavor after a minute or two. You and your cigar will bond, like two old friends and letting it go will become a difficult choice.

Once you make the hard decision to part with your smoked cigar, don't squash it out in an ashtray. Mashing a cigar's ashes will send a bitter smell into the air and bother those around you. It's best etiquette to allow a cigar to burn out naturally.

"A man's shoes will tell you if he has money." "His clothes if he has style." "But if you want to know if he's a sport, see if he is wearing a good cigar."
-Nat Sherman

SAYING THE RIGHT THING

Just like your favorite foods, your favorite cigars require the proper adjectives for both understanding and explaining what you like. Similar to the appreciation of fine wines, cigar characteristics and preferences are a matter of personal taste.

The two most common terms are:

Body is the strength or intensity of a cigar

Flavor is the cigar's taste

Just as with most things in life, a cigar smoker's experience and time will define what is a personal favorite.

Experiment and enjoy!

CIGAR STORAGE

All cigars must be stored in a properly humidified environment. Your cigar should be kept at 70-75 percent relative humidity and at a temperature of 70 degrees Fahrenheit.

Along with today's growth in the cigar market have come an abundance of storage choices. Whether you choose a desktop wooden humidor to hold 25 or a custom built walk-in closet humidor with cedar shelving for 1,500, your cigars need the same environment to stay fresh.

"The cigar numbs sorrow and fills the solitary hours with a million gracious images."
-George Sand

GLOSSARY OF CIGAR TERMS

Binder - the leaf that holds the filler together

Blue Mold - fungus that destroys tobacco leaves; hit Cuba in 1980, Dominican Republic in 1984, Honduras and Nicaragua in 1985, Cuba and Honduras in 1995

Bulk or "burro" - the pile of tobacco leaves left to "sweat" prior to fermentation

Bullet - see Punch

Bunch - cylinder of binder and filler leaves that is rolled into the wrapper

Cap - piece of tobacco used to cover the cigar's head

Capo - Spanish term for "cap"

Chaveta - curve-bladed knife used for trimming cigars during construction

Churchill - long, straight, thick cigar; approximately 6 3/4"- 7 7/8", 46-48 ring gauge

GLOSSARY OF CIGAR TERMS
CONTINUED

Claro - very light tan wrapper leaf, primarily grown in Connecticut

Cohiba - Renowned brand of cigar originating in Cuba, but also manufactured in the Dominican Republic. The word "cohiba" was the Taino Indians' word for "cigar."

Colorado - reddish brown wrapper leaf

Corona - straight, thick cigar; approximately 5 1/4"-5 3/4", 40-44 ring gauge

Cuban Sandwich - cigar made with a combination of long and short filler

Culebra - Cigar constructed of three thin cigars twisted together. Originally given to rollers in Cuban factories to prevent theft of other cigars.

Cutter - device used to clip the head of the cigar to allow air and smoke to pass through

E.M.S. - "English Market Selection," the medium brown wrapper leaf preferred in Britain. Also called "Natural" or "Colorado Claro."

GLOSSARY OF CIGAR TERMS
CONTINUED

Fermentation - two-stage process during which tobacco leaves achieve the desired color and acidity

Filler - the innermost leaves of the cigar

Foot - end of the cigar that is lit

Guillotine - special type of cigar cutter

Hand - also known as "manojo"; a bundle of five wrapper leaves tied together for curing

Handmade - also known as hand-rolled; a cigar bunched, rolled and cut entirely by hand

Head - the end of the cigar that is cut and put in the mouth

Hecho a Mano - Spanish term for "handmade"

Homogenized Binder - binder that is made of tobacco remnants held together with glue or other substances as opposed to a single, whole leaf

GLOSSARY OF CIGAR TERMS
CONTINUED

Humidor - box with a humidification device used for storing cigars

Lectore - cigar factory worker who reads news and literature to the rollers

Ligero - robust leaves from the top of the tobacco plant; slow-burning, they are used for filler

Long Filler - cigar whose filler is made entirely of single leaves bunched together

Lonsdale - straight, medium cigar; approximately 6 1/2"-7 1/4", 40-44 ring gauge

Machine Made - mass-produced cigars made entirely by machines

Maduro - very dark brown or black wrapper leaf grown in Mexico, Nicaragua, Brazil and Connecticut; color category includes Oscuro wrappers (see below)

Oscuro - deep black wrapper leaf

Panatela - straight, thin cigar; approximately 5 1/2"-6 7/8", 35-39 ring gauge

GLOSSARY OF CIGAR TERMS
CONTINUED

Premium - a handmade, long filler cigar

Punch - also called a "bullet"; a cutter that makes a small round hole in the cap of the cigar

Puro - Spanish for cigar

Pyramid - cigar shape that flares along its length from a narrow head to a wider foot

Ring Gauge - thickness of a cigar as measured in 1/64" increments

Robusto - straight, short, thick cigar, also known as "Rothschild"; 4"-5 1/2", 48-54 ring gauge

Seco - light colored leaves from the center of the tobacco plant

Shade - cover (or "tapado") of gauze, linen or silk erected over tobacco plants whose leaves are grown for wrappers. Also a reference to "Connecticut shade" wrappers, or to the color of any wrapper leaf.

GLOSSARY OF CIGAR TERMS
CONTINUED

Short Filler - cigar whose filler is made of remnants and small pieces of tobacco rather than longer, whole leaves

Stogie - now a generic term for any cheap cigar, originally a moniker for cigars made in Conestoga, Pennsylvania, home of the famous frontier wagons

Torcedor - a worker who rolls cigars

Torpedo - thick, tapered cigar made in most standard lengths, 50-60 ring gauge at its thickest

Volado - leaves of the tobacco plant nearest to the ground, often used as binder

Vuelta Abajo - tobacco-growing region in western Cuba, considered the finest land in the world for growing tobacco

Wrapper - outer leaf of the cigar, it holds the binder and filler